An Attachment-Based Model of Parental Alienation: Professional Consultation

C.A. Childress, Psy.D.

An Attachment-Based Model of Parental Alienation: Professional Consultation

Oaksong Press. Claremont, California

Copyright © 2015 Craig Childress

Printed in the United States of America

ISBN 978-0-9961145-3-0

All Rights Reserved.

Contents

Introduction   1

Chapter 1   3

Chapter 2   11

Chapter 3   36

Introduction

This booklet is intended as a structured consultation for mental health professionals in support of parents who believe that their family is evidencing a specific form of pathology that represents a "special population" of children and families who require specialized professional knowledge and expertise to appropriately assess, diagnose, and treat. The specific features of this pathology involve the trans-generational transmission of attachment trauma of one parent to the child, mediated by the narcissistic and/or borderline personality processes of this parent that are significantly distorting family relationships following a divorce.

This booklet is being provided to these parents within the framework of Standard 3.09 of the Ethical Principles of Psychologists and Code of Conduct of the American Psychological Association (2002) regarding Cooperation with Other Professionals, which states,

> When indicated and professionally appropriate, psychologists cooperate with other professionals in order to serve their clients/patients effectively and appropriately. (p. 6)

In this booklet, I am essentially acting as a psychologist consultant to these parents and families regarding their concerns, and this booklet represents my outreach to you as a diagnosing and treating mental health professional to explain the concerns of these parents and ask for your cooperation in assessing the domains of pathology that are of concern.

The special features of the pathology about which this parent is concerned would define this particular client and client family as a "special population" requiring specialized professional knowledge and expertise to appropriately assess, diagnose, and treat, and would activate Standard 2.01a of the Ethical Principles of Psychologists and Code of Conduct of the American Psychological Association (2002) regarding Boundaries of Competence, which states,

> Psychologists provide services, teach and conduct research with populations and in areas only within the boundaries of their competence, based on their education, training, supervised experience, consultation, study or professional experience. (p. 4)

This booklet is being provided as a structured consultation to alert other mental health professionals to the potentially special features involved with this particular client and client family that may warrant specialized assessment for specific diagnostic features, and specialized expertise in treatment. This structured consultation is being offered in the spirit of Standard 3.09 encouraging inter-professional consultation and Standard 2.03 regarding Maintaining Competence which states, "Psychologists undertake ongoing efforts to develop and maintain their competence." (p. 5)

Chapter 1

The Trauma Pathology

The special features that are possibly evident with this client and client family involve the psychological decompensation of a narcissistic and/or borderline personality structure of one of the parents into a delusional belief system regarding the perceived "abusive" parenting practices of the other parent, who is actually a normal-range and affectionally available parent. The formation of delusional beliefs in the narcissistic/borderline parent is the product of the reactivation of childhood attachment trauma (which was responsible for the formation of the narcissistic/borderline personality structures) and the subsequent misinterpretation of elevated anxiety surrounding the threatened collapse of the narcissistic/borderline personality structure and the re-experiencing of childhood relationship trauma as a result of the interpersonal rejection inherent to the divorce.

The threatened collapse of the narcissistic/borderline personality structure and the reactivation of the childhood attachment trauma was triggered by the divorce, which represents the rejection and abandonment of the narcissistic/borderline spouse by the attachment figure because of the judged inadequacy of the narcissistic/borderline spouse. The divorce and loss of the attachment figure of the other spouse activated the attachment system of the narcissistic/borderline parent to mediate this loss experience, and in doing so the divorce experience reactivated the "internal working models" of attachment (Bowlby, 1969, 1973, 1980) – alternately referred to as schemas (Beck, et al. 2004) – that are contained within the narcissistic/borderline parent's attachment system. These internal working models of attachment are highly distorted by the childhood attachment trauma of the narcissistic/borderline parent that produced the narcissistic and borderline personality traits of this person. The representational networks embedded within the attachment system for this childhood attachment trauma are in the pattern of "abusive parent"/"victimized child"/"protective parent."[1]

As a result of the divorce and the re-activation of trauma networks in the attachment system of the narcissistic/borderline parent, two sets of representational networks for attachment figures became concurrently co-activated within the attachment system of the narcissistic/borderline parent; one set representing the current attachment figures of the ex-spouse, the current child, and the current self-representation for the narcissistic/borderline parent, and another set from the internal working models of the narcissistic/borderline parent's attachment networks representing the childhood attachment trauma pattern of "abusive parent"/"victimized child"/"protective parent."

The concurrent co-activation of two sets of representational networks in the attachment system of the narcissistic/borderline parent creates a psychological equivalency in these representational networks. This psychological equivalency of current relationships to childhood representational patterns results in a fusion of perception in which past relationship patterns from childhood are overlaid upon current family relationships. In therapy, when this

---

[1] The split representation for the parent in the internal working models of the narcissistic/borderline parent's attachment system is the result of the splitting dynamic associated with the formation of both narcissistic and borderline personality structures. The all-bad "abusive parent" representational networks are organized around one set of highly negative and frightening childhood relationship experiences, while an entirely separate (split off) set of representational networks are organized around the childhood experiences of the idealized "protective parent," which creates dichotomous and polarized perceptions of attachment figures as either all-good and idealized or as all-bad and demonized (i.e., splitting).

type of psychological equivalency of representational networks is enacted within the patient-therapist relationship it is called "the transference." When childhood trauma is reenacted using people in the general population it is referred to as a "trauma reenactment" (Pearlman & Courtois 2005; Trippany, Helm, & Simpson, 2006; van der Kolk, 1987). According to van der Kolk (1987),

> Victims of trauma respond to contemporary stimuli as if the trauma had returned, without conscious awareness that past injury rather than current stress is the basis of their physiologic emergency responses… People who have been exposed to highly stressful stimuli develop long-term potentiation of memory tracts that are reactivated at times of subsequent arousal. This activation explains how current stress is experienced as a return of the trauma; it causes a return to earlier behavior patterns. (p. 226).

Bowlby (1980) describes the influence of our internal working models of attachment upon our subsequent interpretations of events,

> Every situation we meet within life is construed in terms of the representational models we have of the world about us and of ourselves. Information reaching our sense organs is selected and interpreted in terms of those models, its significance for us and for those we care for is evaluated in terms of them, and plans of action conceived and executed with those models in mind. (p. 229)

In discussing the trans-generational transmission of trauma, Prager describes the recreation of earlier trauma experiences,

> Trauma, as a wound that never heals, succeeds in transforming the subsequent world into its own image, secure in its capacity to re-create the experience for time immemorial. It succeeds in passing the experience from one generation to the next. (Prager, 2003, p. 176)

Pearlman and Courtois (2005) describe the trauma reenactment process and the typical patterns of relationship displayed in the trauma reenactment narrative,

> Reenactments of the traumatic past are common in the treatment of this population and frequently represent either explicit or coded repetitions of the unprocessed trauma in an attempt at mastery. Reenactments can be expressed psychologically, relationally, and somatically and may occur with conscious intent or with little awareness. One primary transference-countertransference dynamic involves reenactment of familiar roles of victim-perpetrator-rescuer-bystander in the therapy relationship. Therapist and client play out these roles, often in complementary fashion with one another, as they relive various aspects of the client's early attachment relationships. (p. 455)

While the narcissistic and borderline personality structures can maintain a veneer of stability in superficial social encounters, the actual narcissistic/borderline personality structure is extremely fragile, especially in response to real or imagined rejection and abandonment by the attachment figure. The interpersonal rejection and abandonment by the spousal attachment figure that is inherent to divorce hits directly on the psychological vulnerabilities of the narcissistic/borderline personality structure. One of the preeminent experts in personality disorders, Theodore Millon, describes the psychological decompensation of the narcissistic personality structure into delusional beliefs in response to stress;

> Under conditions of unrelieved adversity and failure, narcissists may decompensate into paranoid disorders. Owing to their excessive use of fantasy mechanisms, they are disposed to misinterpret events and to construct delusional beliefs. Unwilling to accept constraints on their independence and unable to accept the viewpoints of others, narcissists may isolate themselves from the corrective effects of shared thinking. Alone, they may ruminate and weave their beliefs into a network of fanciful and totally invalid suspicions. Among narcissists, delusions often take form after a serious challenge or setback has upset their image of superiority and omnipotence. They tend to exhibit compensatory grandiosity and jealousy delusions in which they reconstruct reality to match the image they are unable or unwilling to give up. Delusional systems may also develop as a result of having felt

betrayed and humiliated. Here we may see the rapid unfolding of persecutory delusions and an arrogant grandiosity characterized by verbal attacks and bombast. (Millon, 20011, 407-408).

The concurrent co-activation of two sets of representational networks, one for the current family members and a corresponding set contained in the internal working models of the narcissistic/borderline parent's attachment system creates a neurologically based psychological equivalency in these two representational networks in which past and present become fused in the decompensating delusional beliefs of the narcissistic/borderline parent. The psychological correspondence of two sets of representational networks in the attachment system of the narcissistic/borderline parent, one for the current family members and one from the representational networks contained in the internal working models of the attachment system, leads the narcissistic/borderline parent to perceive current relationship through the lens of past trauma (Beck et al, 2004; Bowlby, 1980; van der Kolk, 1987), and to then reenact through the current family relationships the childhood trauma that created the narcissistic and borderline personality structures (Pearlman & Courtois, 2005; Prager, 2003).

In the distorted perceptions of the narcissistic/borderline parent, the current targeted parent takes on the identity of the "abusive parent" representations contained in the internal working models of attachment trauma. The current child becomes the vulnerable "victimized child" of the narcissistic/borderline parent's childhood attachment trauma, and the trauma reenactment role of the idealized and all-wonderful "protective parent" is adopted and then conspicuously displayed by the narcissistic/borderline parent to the "bystanders" comprised of the mental health professionals, attorneys, and judges, whose role is to validate the legitimacy of the trauma reenactment narrative.

In the pathology of the narcissistic/borderline parent, the interpretations of present relationships are altered to reflect the patterns of past childhood trauma. Arron Beck and his colleagues describe the role of schemas (equivalent to Bowlby's concept of "internal working models") in the processing of information,

> How a situation is evaluated depends in part, at least, on the relevant underlying beliefs. These beliefs are embedded in more or less stable structures, labeled "schemas," that select and synthesize incoming data... The content of the schemas may deal with personal relationships, such as attitudes toward the self or others, or impersonal categories. When schemas are latent, they are not participating in information processing; when activated they channel cognitive processing from the earliest to the final stages. (Beck et al., 2004, p. 17; 27)

Roles in the Trauma Reenactment Narrative

The concurrent co-activation of two sets of representational networks in the attachment system of the narcissistic/borderline parent create a psychological fusion of these representational networks in which the perception of current family members becomes distorted by the activated schemas contained within the attachment trauma networks of the narcissistic/borderline parent. As a result, a trauma reenactment narrative is created involving the current family members in which the patterns of the childhood attachment trauma of the narcissistic/borderline parent are imposed on current family members who are then used to recreate the roles embedded in the representational networks of the childhood attachment trauma:

"Abusive Parent" → Targeted Parent

> The representational network for the "abusive parent" in the internal working models of the narcissistic/borderline parent's attachment system is imposed on the targeted parent in the trauma reenactment narrative once the child is induced into adopting the "victimized child" role.

"Victimized Child" → Current Child

> The current child is induced into accepting and adopting the "victimized child" role in the trauma reenactment through the distorted and manipulative relationship and communication practices of the narcissistic/(borderline) parent.

"Protective Parent" → Narcissistic/Borderline Parent

> The "victimized child" role adopted by the child, and the "abusive parent" role that the child's role automatically imposes on the targeted parent, allow the narcissistic/borderline parent to then adopt and conspicuously display to the child and to others the coveted role as the ideal and all-wonderful nurturing and "protective parent."

None of this trauma reenactment narrative is true. The child is not victimized, the targeted parent is not abusive, and the narcissistic/borderline parent is not a protective parent. It is all a false drama created by the narcissistic/borderline parent as a reenactment of childhood trauma patterns contained within the attachment system of the narcissistic/borderline parent. It is a delusion – i.e., it is a fixed and false belief that is maintained despite contrary evidence, consistent with the psychological decompensation of the narcissistic personality into delusional beliefs described by Millon (2011).

The particular concern of the parent who is providing you with this booklet is that the other parent, the allied parent who is supposedly "favored" by the child (i.e., the supposedly all-wonderful "protective parent"), is believed to have prominent narcissistic and/or borderline personality traits that are decompensating after the divorce into delusional beliefs regarding the supposedly "abusive" parenting practices of the targeted parent. The concern of the parent who is being targeted by the delusional beliefs of the narcissistic/borderline parent is that this false belief system of the narcissistic/borderline parent is being transferred to the child through the aberrant and distorted communication and parenting practices of the narcissistic/borderline parent with the child.

The currently targeted-rejected parent is concerned that without proper professional experience and expertise in recognizing the narcissistic and borderline personality processes being expressed within the family, as well as the delusional belief systems and the trauma reenactment narrative, mental health professionals who are involved with this family may not recognize the severity of the pathology and may not accurately diagnose and treat the nature and extent of the pathology involved in this specific family. The parent who is presenting you with this booklet is therefore wanting to alert you to the complexity of this potential pathology that may be involved with this family, and is asking that you please assess for the specific domains of pathology described in the booklet, and which are more fully described and elaborated in the book *Foundations* (Childress, 2015).

    Through this booklet I am acting as a professional consultant to this parent in explaining the nature and extent of the potential pathology involved in this family. On behalf of this parent I am also asking that you assess specifically for this pathology and document in the patient record the results of your assessment as requested by this parent.

Chapter 2

Inducing the Child's Symptoms

The challenge for families following divorce is to successfully transition from an intact family structure that was previously united by the marriage, to a new *separated family structure* that is now united by the children through the continuing parent-child bonds of shared affection and the parental role relationships with the children. In this family, however, the pathology of the narcissistic/borderline parent is being expressed through pathogenic[2] parenting practices that are preventing the family's successful transition to a *separated family structure* following the divorce.

The interpersonal rejection inherent to divorce challenges the fragile personality vulnerabilities of the narcissistic/borderline parent surrounding the experience of primal self-inadequacy and intense fears of abandonment. In order to stabilize the fragile narcissistic/borderline personality structure of the pathological parent, the narcissistic/borderline parent triangulates the child into the spousal conflict through the formation of a cross-generational coalition with the child against the other parent (Haley, 1977; Minuchin, 1974). Within the family systems literature, Jay Haley refers to this cross-generational coalition as a

---

[2] Patho=pathology; genic=genesis, creation. Pathogenic parenting refers to parenting practices that are so aberrant and distorted that they are creating significant psychopathology in the child.

"perverse triangle" while Salvador Minuchin refers to it as a form of "rigid triangle." Haley (1977) provides the following definition for the construct of a cross-generational coalition:

> The people responding to each other in the triangle are not peers, but one of them is of a different generation from the other two... In the process of their interaction together, the person of one generation forms a coalition with the person of the other generation against his peer. By 'coalition' is meant a process of joint action which is *against* the third person... The coalition between the two persons is denied. That is, there is certain behavior which indicates a coalition which, when it is queried, will be denied as a coalition... In essence, the perverse triangle is one in which the separation of generations is breached in a covert way. When this occurs as a repetitive pattern, the system will be pathological. (p. 37)

Salvador Minuchin also describes the cross-generational coalition and provides a specific case example of the impact on family relationships from a cross-generational coalition following divorce;

> The rigid triangle can also take the form of a stable coalition. One of the parents joins the child in a rigidly bounded cross-generational coalition against the other parent. (Minuchin, 1974, p. 102)

> The parents were divorced six months earlier and the father is now living alone... Two of the children who were very attached to their father, now refuse any contact with him. The younger children visit their father but express great unhappiness with the situation. (Minuchin, 1974, p. 101)

The "perverse triangle" created by a cross-generational coalition reflects a role-reversal relationship in which the child is being used as a "regulatory object" to stabilize and regulate the emotional and psychological state of the psychologically fragile parent. The parent in a cross-generational coalition is using (exploiting) the child's induced and parentally supported hostility and rejection toward the other parent to re-route through the child the spousal anger that the allied parent has toward the targeted parent.

A cross-generational coalition of a parent with a child against the other parent is always pathological. But when the allied and supposedly "favored" parent also has narcissistic and borderline personality traits, the cross-generational coalition with the child takes on particularly vicious and malignant form in which the child seeks to entirely terminate a relationship with the other parent. This transformation in the malignancy of the cross-generational coalition is created by the addition of "splitting" pathology to the cross-generational coalition.

The pathology of "splitting" is associated with both narcissistic and borderline personality processes and involves a polarized perception of relationships into extremes of all-good or all-bad. The psychological process of splitting is unable to accommodate to ambiguity in relationships (Juni, 1995) and so creates polarized perceptions of people and relationships. For the narcissistic/borderline parent following divorce, when the husband or wife became an ex-husband or an ex-wife, they must also then become an ex-parent as well because nuanced ambiguity in the perception of role-relationships is impossible for the splitting dynamic to accommodate.[3] The pathology of the spitting dynamic eliminates ambiguity by imposing a rigid

---

[3] The psychopathology of splitting represents an excessive and complete neurological cross-inhibition of the attachment bonding and avoidance motivational networks. When one motivational system is active, the other system is entirely shut down (cross-inhibited). When the spouse becomes an ex-spouse the representational networks for the now ex-spouse switch from the attachment bonding motivational system to the avoidance motivating system. The activation of the avoidance motivating system will then entirely cross-inhibit the attachment bonding motivational system. The complete cross-inhibition of the attachment-bonding motivational networks means that the narcissistic/borderline parent can no longer perceptually register the child's continuing bonds of affection with the now ex-spouse (attachment motivating networks) because these networks are being entirely cross-inhibited by the "spitting" occurring in the neurological networks of the narcissistic/borderline parent.

consistency onto the perception of relationships. The psychological consistency imposed by the pathology of splitting <u>requires</u> that the ex-husband also become an ex-father; that the ex-wife must also become an ex-mother. The neurobiological basis for the splitting dynamic allows no other alternative. The addition of the splitting pathology to the cross-generational coalition transmutes an already pathological parent-child coalition into a particularly malignant form in which the child seeks to entirely terminate the other parent's relationship with the child, so that the ex-husband of the narcissistic/borderline parent also becomes an ex-father; the ex-wife an ex-mother.

Creating the Role-Reversal Relationship

The means by which the cross-generational coalition is created involves a complex set of manipulative communication practices by the narcissistic/borderline parent that have as their foundation the formation of a role-reversal relationship with the child in which the child is used as a "regulatory object" by the parent to stabilize the emotional and psychological state regulation of the narcissistic/borderline parent. The process of inducing the child into becoming a "regulatory object" for the narcissistic/borderline parent is incredibly easy. The narcissistic and borderline personality is exceptionally skilled at manipulative communication, and the child's immaturity makes an easy target for the sophisticated manipulative communications of the narcissistic/borderline parent.

The volatile emotionality and intense anger of the narcissistic/borderline personality motivates the child to act and respond in ways that maintain the stability of the parent's emotional and psychological state. If the child reads cues from the narcissistic/borderline parent and responds in the ways desired by the parent, then the emotional and psychological state of the narcissistic/borderline parent remains organized and regulated. If, however, the child responds to parental cues in non-desired ways, then the emotional and psychological regulation of the narcissistic/borderline parent collapses into displays of narcissistic rage, irrational accusations, borderline anger, and volatile displays of tearful victimization. The child quickly learns the types of responses needed to keep the narcissistic/borderline parent in a regulated emotional and psychological state, and which types of responses to avoid.

The unstable psychological state and emotional volatility of the narcissistic/borderline parent motivates the child to continually monitor the psychological state of the parent in order to respond in ways that keep the unstable parent in an organized and regulated state (Rappoport, 2005). By continually monitoring the psychological state of the parent and by providing responses that stabilize the emotional and psychological state of the narcissistic/borderline parent, the child becomes an external "regulatory object" for the parent.

This type of relationship, in which the child is used as a "regulatory object" for the parent, represents a role-reversal relationship in which the child is meeting the needs of the parent. In the child's role-reversal relationship as the "regulatory object" for the emotional and psychological state of the parent, the child is tasked with preventing the collapse of the narcissistic/borderline parent into punitive displays of excessive anger and sadness. The emotional instability and volatility of the narcissistic/borderline parent induces and shapes the child's interactions with this parent into expressing what the narcissistic/borderline parent wants and needs in order to keep the unstable parent in an emotionally and psychologically regulated state.

Through distorted relationship and communication dynamics, the narcissistic/borderline parent then nullifies the child's authenticity and replaces it with a reflection of the narcissistic/borderline parent's own attitudes, beliefs, and psychological state. As noted by Rappoport (2005),

> In a narcissistic encounter, there is, psychologically, only one person present. The co-narcissist disappears for both people, and only the narcissistic person's experience is important. (p. 3)

In the *Journal of Emotional Abuse*, Kerig (2005) describes the process by which a parent psychologically controls and manipulates the child's very authenticity, and the subsequent impact on the child's emotional and psychological development resulting from the pathology of the role-reversal relationship,

> Rather than telling the child directly what to do or think, as does the behaviorally controlling parent, the psychologically controlling parent uses indirect hints and responds with guilt induction or withdrawal of love if the child refuses to comply. In short, an intrusive parent strives to manipulate the child's thoughts and feelings in such a way that the child's psyche will conform to the parent's wishes. (p. 12)

> In order to carve out an island of safety and responsivity in an unpredictable, harsh, and depriving parent-child relationship, children of highly maladaptive parents may become precocious caretakers who are adept at reading the cues and meeting the needs of those around them. The ensuing preoccupied attachment with the parent interferes with the child's development of important ego functions, such as self organization, affect regulation, and emotional object constancy. (p. 14)

Inducing the "Victimized Child"

The narcissistic/borderline parent does not induce the child's hostile rejection of the other parent by overtly and directly denigrating the other parent (although such denigration does occur). Instead the child's hostility (or excessive anxiety)[4] and rejection of the other parent is created by first inducing the child into accepting the role as the "victimized child" in the trauma reenactment narrative. Once the child adopts the "victimized child" role, this immediately imposes on the targeted parent the (false) role as the "abusive parent" in the trauma reenactment narrative. The key lynchpin in creating the pathology is inducing the child into adopting the "victimized child" role in the trauma reenactment narrative of "abusive parent"/"victimized child"/"protective parent." Once the child adopts the "victimized

---

[4] The narcissistic-style parent tends to induce child hostility toward the other parent whereas the more borderline-style parent tends to induce excessive displays of child anxiety and fearfulness regarding the targeted parent.

child" role, this automatically defines the other two trauma reenactment roles of the "abusive parent" (the targeted-rejected parent) and the "protective parent" (the narcissistic/borderline) parent.

Since the child is acting as a "regulatory object" for the narcissistic/borderline parent's emotional and psychological state, it is relatively easy to then induce the child into accepting and adopting the "victimized child" role within the trauma reenactment narrative. This is accomplished by first eliciting from the child a criticism of the other parent through motivated and subtly directive parental questioning. This criticism of the other parent, elicited from the child by the subtle but clearly directive questioning of the narcissistic/borderline parent, is then inflamed and distorted by the response this elicited child criticism of the other parent receives from the narcissistic/borderline parent. The response of the narcissistic/borderline parent to the child's (subtly elicited) criticism of the other parent distorts and inflames the criticism into supposed evidence of the other parent's "abusive" insensitivity to the child, and for supposed character flaws in the other parent that justify the child's hostility toward that parent.

> **Narcissistic/Borderline Parent:** "How did things go at your mother's house? Did you two get along?"
>
> <an invitation for the criticism of the other parent>
>
> **Child:** "Yeah, it was okay."
>
> <the child ignores the invitation>
>
> **N/B Parent:** "Really? You guys got along okay? There weren't any arguments or anything?"
>
> <the narcissistic/borderline parent continues to seek the criticism through subtly directive questioning>
>
> **Child:** "Well, she got upset with me for leaving some of my stuff in the living room."
>
> <the child provides the parent with the desired criticism>

[17]

N/B Parent: "Oh my God, really? She got mad at you for that? I can't believe her, everything has to be her way or she'll fly into one of her rages. I hate when she does that. It's as if you're just a guest over there and you don't live there too. I can't believe how controlling she is. Well, I'm sorry you have to put up with that from her. I wish she wasn't like that. But you're home now and you can relax."

In this distorted and manipulative communication exchange the narcissistic/borderline parent inflames the child's relatively innocuous criticism describing a normal-range parent-child interaction into supposed evidence of the mother's character flaws and insensitivity to the child. This distorted inflammation of the child's initial (and elicited) criticism creates a definition of the child as being "victimized" by the supposedly "abusive" insensitivity of the other parent to the child's needs.

Yet the external appearance of this manipulative exchange is that the child is "independently" criticizing the other parent, even though the child's criticism of the other parent was elicited by motivated and directive questioning of the narcissistic/borderline parent. By first eliciting the criticism of the other parent from the child, the response of the narcissistic/borderline parent can be portrayed as simply being a nurturing and supportive "protective parent" for the child. The narcissistic/borderline parent is hiding the manipulation of the child behind the child's elicited criticism of the other parent. This role-reversal use of the child in which the motivated and directive questioning of the narcissistic/borderline parent first elicits and then distorts a criticism from the child regarding the other parent, is used to place the child out front into the leadership position of criticizing the other parent in order to allow the narcissistic/borderline parent to hide the parental manipulation of the child through the distorted communication practices of the narcissistic/borderline parent. This role-reversal use of the child is expressed by the narcissistic/borderline parent in the joint themes, "It's not me, it's the child" and "We need to listen to the child."

N/B Parent: "It's not me, it's the child. I'm not criticizing the other parent. It's the child who's criticizing the other parent.

I'm just listening to the child. You should listen to the child. It's not me, it's the child. We need to listen to the child."

These two themes, "It's not me, it's the child" and "We need to listen to the child" reflect the role-reversal manipulation and exploitation of the child by a narcissistic/borderline parent, and are particularly characteristic of this pathology.

In the distorted communication exchanges that define the child as being "victimized" by the supposedly insensitive and "abusive" parenting practices of the other parent, the narcissistic/borderline parent is also able to communicate to the child a set of acceptable "themes" that the child can use for criticizing the other parent. In the case of the preceding example, the themes provided to the child for criticizing the other parent are that "everything has to be her way or she'll fly into one of her rages" and about "how controlling she is." These seemingly "supportive" statements by the narcissistic/borderline parent actually extend and elaborate on the child's (elicited) criticism by providing general themes for criticizing the other parent. Yet throughout this process, a superficial appearance is maintained that it is the child who is "independently" criticizing the other parent and that the narcissistic/borderline parent is simply being "supportive" of the child ("It's not me, it's the child. I'm just listening to the child. You should listen to the child. The child will tell you. It's not me, it's the child.").

Through repeated enactments of these distorted communication exchanges, the "regulatory object" of the child comes to learn what is expected of him or her in these exchanges, and begins to more actively participate in fulfilling his or her role in these exchanges of providing the narcissistic/borderline parent with criticisms of the other parent. As an attuned "regulatory object" for the parent, the child realizes that the more extreme the criticisms of the other parent are the more they please the narcissistic/borderline parent, who subtly but clearly communicates this parental pleasure to the child. The child also learns that truth and accuracy are less important than vitriol. Eventually, the child will embrace the role of the "victimized child" in these communication exchanges, and the child will begin to offer fully-voiced criticisms of the other parent.

> **N/B Parent:** "How were things at your mother's house? Did everything go okay?"
>
> **Child:** "No. I hate it over there. Everything always has to be her way or she'll get so angry. She has to control every little thing. I hate it over there."
>
> **N/B Parent:** "I'm so sorry she's like that. You poor thing, having to put up with her. I wish she wasn't like that. It must be awful for you having to put up with her. I know just what you're going through. She was just like that with me during our marriage. But you're home now and you can relax and take it easy. Hey, would you like me to fix you a snack?"

By adopting the acceptable "themes" for criticizing the other parent, the child is relieved from the burden of having to come up with specific incidents for these "bash the parent" exchanges. Instead, the child can simply rely on a set of pre-established generalized criticisms. These general themes will often be reiterated in therapy as justification for the child's hostility and rejection of the targeted parent, with the child adopting and displaying for the therapist the "victimized child" role co-created and rehearsed with the narcissistic/borderline parent. In therapy, the child will offer general criticisms regarding the supposed insensitivity of the targeted parent to what the child wants and feels, and the child will use this general criticism as justification for rejecting the targeted parent. If a therapist seeks additional reports from the child regarding specific incidents, these additional descriptions will reveal the child's sense of grandiose <u>entitlement</u> (acquired though the distorting influence of the narcissistic/borderline parent), or the child will resort to reporting on one or two prior incidents of a supposedly "unforgivable event" which the child then uses to justify all current and future hostility and rejection of the targeted parent.

Once the child psychologically surrenders into becoming the "regulatory object" for meeting the needs of the narcissistic/(borderline) parent, the child is secure in the stability of the emotional and psychological state of the narcissistic/borderline parent. These "bash the parent" exchanges not only serve to stabilize the psychological and emotional functioning of the narcissistic/borderline parent, they also strengthen the fragile bond (insecure attachment) that the child has with the emotionally unstable borderline-style parent or emotionally distant narcissistic-style parent. These "bash the parent" exchanges strengthen the child's fragile (conditional) attachment bond to the narcissistic/borderline parent by highlighting their shared bond of mutual "victimization" from the "abuse" supposedly being inflicted on both of them by the other parent (us-versus-them). In describing the formation of the parent-child coalition, Juni (1995) observes how "the sharing of hate feelings toward an object serves to cement a positive alliance" (p. 101).

When the child psychologically surrenders into accepting and adopting the "victimized child" role, it is only a small step to then extend the child's supposed "victimization" into an entitled sense of judgement, hostility, and rejection of the other parent for that parent's supposedly "abusive" insensitivity to the child's emotional needs. When the child eventually surrenders to the role as the "victimized child," the narcissistic/borderline parent is then able to exploit the child's induced "victimization," hostility, and rejection of the other parent to meet the psychological need of the narcissistic/borderline parent to turn the ex-spouse into an ex-parent. By exploiting the child's induced symptoms of supposed "victimization," hostility, and rejection of the other parent, the narcissistic/borderline parent is able to achieve the goal of nullifying the other parent's parental rights and relationship with the child, irrespective of court orders and the actual parenting practices of the other parent, which is a goal that would otherwise be unattainable if the narcissistic/borderline parent tried to achieve it directly without first manipulating the child into a role-reversal relationship of rejecting the other parent.

Through the role-reversal relationship, the narcissistic/borderline parent is first inducing pathology in the child in order to then exploit the child's pathology to meet the emotional and psychological needs of the narcissistic/borderline parent. This process of manipulating and exploiting the child in order to meet the needs of the parent reflects the distinctive personality disorder traits of manipulation and exploitation characteristic of the narcissistic/borderline personality:

- By first manipulating the child into becoming the "regulatory object" for the emotional and psychological state of the parent, the narcissistic/borderline parent is then able to manipulate the child into accepting and displaying the role as the supposedly "victimized child" relative to the other parent.

- By manipulating the child into adopting the leadership position of criticizing and rejecting the other parent, the narcissistic/borderline parent is able to exploit the child's induced role as the "victimized child" - and the child's induced hostility and rejection of the targeted parent - to nullify the other parent's visitation and affectionally bonded relationship with the child, thereby turning the ex-spouse into an ex-parent (as required by the splitting dynamic).

- The narcissistic/borderline parent then exploits the child's induced role as the "victimized child" and the child's rejection of the other parent to manipulate mental health professionals into becoming allies of the pathology in order to confer legitimacy to the false trauma reenactment narrative of the child's supposed "victimization" by the supposedly "abusive" parenting by the other parent.

- The narcissistic/borderline parent exploits the collusion of naïve mental health allies with the pathology to nullify court orders for joint visitation and custody by replacing the child's visitations with the other parent with ineffective "reunification therapy."

- If the therapist recognizes the pathology and does not accept the child's artificially created role as the "victimized child," then the narcissistic/borderline parent will elicit from the child, by means of the child's role-reversal relationship and the subtly directive questioning of the parent, criticisms of the therapist that "the child doesn't feel understood" by the therapist because "the therapist isn't listening to the child." The narcissistic/borderline parent will then covertly manipulate the "regulatory object" of the child into refusing to attend therapy, and will use the child's (elicited) refusal to attend therapy to terminate therapy with the mental health professional who is not cooperating with the trauma reenactment narrative.

> **N/B Parent:** "What can I do? I can't force the child to attend therapy. It's not me, it's the child. The child doesn't feel understood. The therapist isn't listening to the child. It's not me, it's the child."

The narcissistic/borderline parent will exploit the child's (elicited) criticisms of the therapist and (elicited) refusal to attend therapy to replace the therapist with one who will "listen to the child" and who will confirm the legitimacy of the false trauma reenactment narrative of the child's supposed "victimization" by the supposedly "abusive" parenting of the targeted-rejected parent.

Prominent in this pathology is the pathogenic parenting of the narcissistic/borderline parent that is inducing pathology in the child through a *role-reversal* relationship in order for the narcissistic/borderline parent to then *exploit* the child's symptoms to meet the needs of the narcissistic/borderline parent.

Suppression of Attachment Bonding

The child's attachment bonding motivations toward the other parent, which are normally a strong and resilient primary motivation for children, can be artificially nullified and suppressed through both the child's chronically maintained anger toward the targeted parent and through parental displays by the narcissistic/borderline parent of hyper-anxious over-concern for the child's supposed "safety" whenever the child is in the care of the other parent. The emotion of anger inhibits the activation of attachment bonding motivations, and chronic anger will maintain a continual inhibitory suppression on the child's attachment bonding motivations.

In addition, parental emotional signals of anxiety will also act to artificially suppress the child's attachment bonding motivations toward the targeted parent by subliminally activating the child's attachment system response to threat. Signals of parental anxiety for the child's "safety" will trigger the child's attachment system to respond in characteristic ways that motivate the child to flee from and avoid the parentally-signaled source of threat and danger to the child. The attachment system is foundationally a predator-driven primary motivational system. In response to parental signals of anxiety regarding the child's safety, the attachment system motivates the child to avoid the parentally identified source of threat and to remain in the continual protective proximity of the "protective parent" (i.e., the parent who is signaling to the child parental anxiety and concern for the child's safety).

The attachment system is a primary motivational system that evolved in response to the selective predation of children (Bowlby, 1969; 1973; 1980). According to Bowlby (1980),

> The biological function of this behavior [attachment behavior] is postulated to be protection, especially protection from predators… Attachment behavior is in no way confined to children. Although usually less readily aroused, we see it also in adolescents and adults of both sexes whenever they are anxious or under stress. (p. 3-4)

Since the evolutionary origins of the attachment system are in the selective targeting of children by predators, the attachment system is highly sensitized to recognizing and responding to parental signals of anxiety and protective concern for the child's safety. When the narcissistic/borderline parent signals parental anxiety and concern for the child's "safety" relative to the other parent, the expressed anxiety of the narcissistic/borderline parent subliminally activates the child's attachment system response to parental signals of threat perception.

The emotional signaling of parental anxiety and concerns for the child's "safety" when the child is with the other parent defines the targeted parent as representing a source of threat to the child (i.e., as being "the predator" relative to the functioning of the child's attachment system). The attachment system does not motivate children to form attachment bonds to the threat (i.e., to "the predator") but instead motivates children to flee from and avoid the parentally identified source of threat and to seek the protection of the "protective parent" who is signaling anxiety and concern for the child's safety. This "protective parent" role is exactly the role being adopted and conspicuously displayed to the child by the narcissistic/borderline parent.

The display of parental anxiety for the child's "safety" with the other parent acts to subliminally define the other parent as representing a source of threat to the child (as being "the predator") relative to the functioning of the child's attachment system, and the parental signals of anxiety also correspondingly define the narcissistic/borderline parent as being the supposedly "protective parent" who is concerned for the child's safety. The child's attachment system, which is highly sensitized by its evolutionary development to register and respond to parental signals of anxiety, will then motivate the child to flee from and avoid "the predator" threat and to instead seek to remain in the continual protective proximity of the concerned and anxious "protective parent."

Creating the Trauma Reenactment Narrative

The narcissistic/borderline parent creates the child's symptomatic rejection of the other parent by manipulating and inducing the child into adopting the "victimized child" role in the trauma reenactment narrative. The moment the child adopts the role as the "victimized child" in the trauma reenactment narrative, this immediately imposes onto the targeted parent the role as the "abusive parent," irrespective of the actual parenting practices of the targeted parent. This represents a masterful display of narcissistic and borderline manipulation and exploitation of the child's induced symptoms. Once the child adopts the "victimized child role, the targeted parent must then continually prove a negative; i.e., that his or her parenting practices are not "abusive" of the child. However, it is nearly impossible to prove a negative, so the focus of accusation and the burden of proof always remains on the targeted parent, and the severe psychopathology of the narcissistic/borderline parent is able to hide behind a constructed presentation as the idealized and all-wonderful, nurturing and "protective parent."

When mental health professionals fail to recognize the extent of the manipulative and exploitative pathology of the narcissistic/borderline parent, they will incorrectly accept the legitimacy of the trauma reenactment narrative and begin to collude in co-constructing the narrative that the child's relationship with targeted parent must somehow be problematic in order to produce the child's hostility and rejection. By placing the targeted parent continually on the defensive of proving a negative (i.e., that his or her parenting is not abusive) the "victimized child" role diverts the focus of mental health professionals away from the pathology of the narcissistic/borderline parent and onto the normal-range parenting of the targeted parent. Meanwhile the pathology of the narcissistic/borderline parent remains hidden behind the role-reversal manipulation and exploitation of the child ("It's not me, it's the child who...xyz") and the "protective parent" role adopted and conspicuously displayed to others by the narcissistic/borderline parent.

But none of this trauma reenactment narrative is true. The child is not a victim, the targeted parent is not abusive, and the narcissistic/borderline parent is not the wonderful protective parent. It is a kabuki theater display of past trauma, and it actuality represents a projective reversal of the truth. The child is actually a victim of manipulative exploitation by the narcissistic/borderline parent. It is the narcissistic/borderline parent who is actually the psychologically abusive parent who is seducing the child into a "perverse" cross-generational coalition that destroys the child's relationship with the other parent (who is actually a normal-range, loving, and affectionally available parent); and it is actually this targeted-rejected parent who is the authentically protective parent. It is the targeted-rejected parent who is trying to protect the child from the pathology of the role-reversal relationship with the narcissistic/borderline parent that is destroying the child's authenticity and childhood. The false trauma reenactment narrative created by the pathology of the narcissistic/borderline parent represents an inverted projection of the truth. Mental health professionals working with this form of pathology must possess an advanced level of expertise in the projective pathology of narcissistic and borderline personality processes as a foundation for their professional competence.

The lynchpin in creating the false and distorted trauma reenactment narrative is inducing the child into believing and adopting the role as the "victimized child." This is accomplished through the formation of a role-reversal relationship in which the child becomes a "regulatory object" for stabilizing the emotional and psychological state of the narcissistic/borderline parent. The moment the child adopts the "victimized child" role in the trauma reenactment narrative, the role of the "abusive parent" is automatically imposed onto the targeted parent, and the narcissistic/borderline parent is allowed to adopt and conspicuously display the role as the ideal and all-wonderful "protective parent."

Projection of Core Vulnerabilities

By inducing the child into judging and rejecting the other parent, the core psychological vulnerabilities of primal self-inadequacy and fear of abandonment are psychologically expelled from the narcissistic/borderline parent onto the other parent by projectively displacing them onto the other parent. The child's judgement and rejection of the other parent defines the targeted parent as being the inadequate parent (and person) who is being rejected and abandoned for this supposed inadequacy as a parent (and as a person). The narcissistic/borderline parent exploits the child's induced rejection of the other parent to projectively displace onto the targeted parent the narcissistic/borderline parent's own self-experience of primal inadequacy and core fear of abandonment that were activated by the rejection and abandonment inherent to the divorce.

Projective Displacement: "I'm not the inadequate parent/(person); you are. And I'm not being abandoned and rejected because of my inadequacy; *you're* being rejected and abandoned because of *your* inadequacy. You're the bad and inadequate parent/(person); not me. I'm the ideal and all-wonderful parent/(person)."

However, this projective displacement onto the other parent of the narcissistic/borderline parent's own primal self-inadequacy and fear of abandonment can only occur if the child appears to be "independently" judging and rejecting the other parent for that parent's supposed inadequacy as a parent (and person). If it is evident that the child's rejection of the other parent is being created by the negative parental influence of the narcissistic/borderline parent then this will not define the targeted parent as being an inadequate and "abusive" parent.

Instead, if it is evident that the child's rejection of the other parent is the product of negative parental influence exercised on the child by the narcissistic/borderline parent, then this will only turn the targeted parent into being a sympathetic victim, rather than a supposedly malicious perpetrator of child abuse that is needed for the trauma reenactment narrative. For the trauma reenactment narrative to fulfill its function of projectively displacing onto the targeted parent the primal fears of self-inadequacy and abandonment, the child must appear to be independently rejecting the targeted parent for that parent's judged inadequacy as a parent (as a person). The negative parental influence on the child by the narcissistic/borderline parent must remain hidden from view, otherwise the roles within the trauma reenactment narrative fall apart.

Allies to Pathology

The drama of "abusive parent"/"victimized child"/"protective parent" enacted in the family is a form of kabuki theater display – a false drama created and displayed for the bystanders of the trauma reenactment. Perlman and Courtois (2005) identify four roles in the trauma reenactment narrative, the "perpetrator," the "victim," the "rescuer," and the "bystander" roles. The primary function of the "bystander" role is to validate the legitimacy of the trauma reenactment narrative; i.e., that the child is a "victim" of the supposedly "abusive" parenting of the inadequate targeted-rejected parent, and that the narcissistic/borderline parent is the all-wonderful and ideal "protective parent."

The trauma reenactment narrative is not true. It is a delusional construction of the narcissistic/borderline parent. But it is granted legitimacy when the "bystanders" represented by the involved therapists, attorneys, and judges accept the trauma reenactment narrative as being authentic. The role of the "bystander" therapists, custody evaluators, attorneys, and judges is to validate and legitimize the (false) trauma reenactment narrative. When this occurs, these "bystanders" in the trauma reenactment are then co-opted by the pathology of the narcissistic/borderline parent into colluding with the pathology.

When mental health professionals fail to recognize the extent and severity of the pathology, they become allies of the pathology within the trauma reenactment narrative. By accepting the kabuki theater display of the trauma reenactment narrative as being legitimate, naïve and unsuspecting mental health professionals will confer legitimacy onto the false and destructive trauma reenactment pathology of the narcissistic/borderline parent, and these mental health professionals will be manipulated into colluding with and supporting the psychopathology that will damage the child's healthy development and destroy the child's relationship with the normal-range and authentically protective targeted parent.

Because this specific pathology presents a false narrative which is supported by the child's presented display of symptoms (which are created through the child's role-reversal relationship with the pathological parent), it is essential for involved mental health professionals to be expert and competent in recognizing, assessing, diagnosing, and treating the component aspects of the pathology. Unless the involved mental health professionals are alert to the nature and severity of the psychopathology, which includes professional expertise in the recognition and assessment of narcissistic and borderline personality processes, then the nature and severity of the psychopathology being expressed in the family can be easily overlooked, and the mental health professional will be co-opted into colluding with the pathology; granting legitimacy to a false and delusional narrative of "abuse" and "victimization."

The kabuki theater display of the trauma reenactment narrative is made even more captivating by the child's insistence that the targeted parent is a bad and "abusive" parent. We are naturally drawn to protect children, and the narrative of the "abusive parent"/"victimized child"/"protective parent" is a commonly encountered reality in mental health. The narrative of abuse and victimization fits with the preconceived expectations of mental health professionals who are unsuspecting of the delusional pathology of the narcissistic and borderline personality process. Unsuspecting and unaware mental health professionals can easily be drawn into accepting and legitimizing the false narrative created by the childhood attachment trauma of the narcissistic/borderline parent. However, when mental health professionals fail to recognize the nature and severity of the actual trauma reenactment pathology, they become allies to the pathology within the family.

The presentation of the narcissistic and borderline personality during superficial clinical encounters can also contribute to the manipulation and exploitation of naïve mental health professionals as allies to the pathology. Both the narcissistic and borderline personalities present well in superficial encounters, and both the narcissistic and borderline personality are highly skilled at manipulation to enlist allies. The narcissistic personality presents as self-confident, calmly serene, and self-assured. It is easy for unsuspecting "bystanders," even mental health professionals, to become seduced by the calmly assertive self-confidence of the narcissistic personality, and so become allies of the narcissistic parent in the kabuki theater of the trauma reenactment narrative.

Millon (2011) describes the presentation of the narcissistic personality,

> When not faced with humiliating or stressful situations, CENs [Confident Egoistic Narcissists] convey a calm and self-assured quality in their social behavior. Their untroubled and self-satisfied air is viewed by some as a sign of confident equanimity. (p. 388-389)

Beck et al. (2004) describe how "narcissists can display a deceptively warm demeanor" (p. 241), and Kernberg (1975) likewise describes the superficially positive presentation of the narcissistic personality,

> Highly intelligent patients with this personality structure may appear as quite creative in their fields: narcissistic personalities can often be found as leaders in industrial organizations or academic institutions; they may also be outstanding performers in some artistic domain. (p. 229)

The outward presentation of the borderline-style personality is also designed to manipulate others and enlist allies. In superficial encounters, the borderline-style personality presents as emotionally vulnerable and in need of protection. The distorted presentation of interpersonal relationships is also highly characteristic of the borderline-style personality,

> In clinical practice and in the literature, patients with borderline personality disorder (BPD) have long had a reputation for distorted thinking about what transpires in their interpersonal relationships... BPD patients often describe others as if they believe others are idealized paragons of perfection or denigrated embodiments of pure malevolence. They often describe interactional sequences in misleading or self-serving ways. They often recount the alleged misdeeds of others while systematically downplaying their own provocative behavior as potential reasons for them. (Bailey & Shriver, 1999, p. 21-22)

The borderline personality's presentation of vulnerability and victimization elicits a nurturing and protective response from others. The borderline personality is extremely adept at manipulation, and the elicited nurturing-protective responses of others are exploited by the borderline-style personality to enlist allies for enacting the pathology. The mental health professional who becomes a "protective ally" for the borderline-style personality is rewarded with displays of gratitude for being the "idealized paragon of perfection," which can, in turn, feed the counter-transference of the therapist.

But the kabuki theater display of the trauma reenactment narrative is not true. The child's relationship with the supposedly "favored" parent actually represents an extremely pathological role-reversal relationship in which the child is being used (exploited) as a "regulatory object" to meet the emotional and psychological needs of a narcissistic or borderline parent. The severe pathology of the role-reversal relationship is described by Kerig (2005),

> The breakdown of appropriate generational boundaries between parents and children significantly increases the risk for emotional abuse… In the throes of their own insecurity, troubled parents may rely on the child to meet the parent's emotional needs, turning to the child to provide the parent with support, nurturance, or comforting. Ultimately, preoccupation with the parents' needs threatens to interfere with the child's ability to develop autonomy, initiative, self-reliance, and a secure internal working model of the self and others… When parent-child boundaries are violated, the implications for developmental psychopathology are significant. Poor boundaries interfere with the child's capacity to progress through development which, as Anna Freud (1965) suggested, is the defining feature of childhood psychopathology. (p. 6-7)

Kerig also notes another distinctive feature of the role-reversal pathology, that "enmeshment in one parent-child relationship is often counterbalanced by disengagement between the child and the other parent" (Kerig, 2005, p. 10). While superficially a role-reversal relationship will appear to be a bonded (enmeshed) parent-child relationship, the violation of psychological boundaries with the child in which the child is used to meet the emotional and psychological needs of the parent actually represents a serious form of parent-child pathology.

Misunderstood and Misattributed Grief

The child's authentic experience involves the misattribution of unprocessed and misinterpreted grief and sadness, first over the loss of the intact family through the parents' divorce, and then at the loss of an affectionally bonded relationship with the beloved-but-now-rejected targeted parent. All children love their parents, even if these parents are problematic and annoying. The attachment bond of a child for a parent is extremely strong and resilient. One of the leading experts in the attachment system, Mary Ainsworth, describes the attachment bond;

> I define an "affectional bond" as a relatively long-enduring tie in which the partner is important as a unique individual and is interchangeable with none other. In an affectional bond, there is a desire to maintain closeness to the partner. In older children and adults, that closeness may to some extent be sustained over time and distance and during absences, but nevertheless there is at least an intermittent desire to reestablish proximity and interaction, and pleasure – often joy – upon reunion. Inexplicable separation tends to cause distress, and permanent loss would cause grief.
>
> An "attachment" is an affectional bond, and hence an attachment figure is never wholly interchangeable with or replaceable by another, even though there may be others to whom one is also attached. In attachments, as in other affectional bonds, there is a need to maintain proximity, distress upon inexplicable separation, pleasure and joy upon reunion, and grief at loss. (Ainsworth, 1989, p. 711)

All children love their parents, both parents, and all children want to be loved by their parents, both parents. For a child to reject a normal-range and affectionally available parent is extremely aberrant and unusual. Children actually become MORE strongly motivated to bond to problematic parents (called an "insecure attachment"). The attachment system is a "goal corrected" primary motivational system (Bowlby, 1969; 1973; 1980) and in response to problematic parenting children will display characteristic patterns of responses that are all designed to

<u>increase</u> parental involvement. Child protest behavior represents a form of "attachment behavior" which has as its goal the formation of an attached bond to the parent. The normal-range and authentic attachment system never displays "detachment behavior" (even a highly problematic parent is still better than the predator).

The attachment system is a very strong and resilient, "goal-corrected" primary motivational system, and there are only a limited number of severely pathogenic circumstances that can terminate a child's attachment bonding motivations toward a parent:

> **Incest:** The child's attachment bonding motivations toward a parent will be terminated in response to parental sexual abuse of the child.
>
> **Chronic and Severe Parental Violence:** Years of chronic and severe parental violence, either in the form of domestic violence against the spouse or physical abuse directed toward the child can sometimes, but not necessarily always, terminate the child's attachment bonding motivations toward the parent.
>
> **Chronic and Severe Parental Incapacity:** Chronic and severe parental incapacity, such as chronic parental alcoholism or drug abuse, can sometimes terminate the child's attachment bonding motivations toward the parent. This termination of the attachment bonding motivation due to chronic and severe parental incapacity reflects the child's profound discouragement at being able to form an attached bond to the parent. If the parent recovers and becomes relationally available to the child, the child's attachment bonding motivations will often be restored.
>
> **Role-Reversal Relationship with a Narcissistic/Borderline Parent:** The formation of a cross-generational coalition of the child with a narcissistic/borderline parent in which the child is used in a role-reversal relationship as a "regulatory object" for the emotional and psychological needs of the narcissistic/borderline parent can induce the artificial

suppression of the child's attachment-bonding motivations toward the other parent. This is the pathology discussed in this booklet and in *Foundations* (Childress, 2015).

Special Population

It is essential for mental health professionals treating this special population of children and families to possess the necessary professional knowledge and expertise in narcissistic and borderline personality disorder pathology (especially the psychological decompensation of narcissistic and borderline personality pathology into delusional belief systems), in the expression of the attachment system during childhood (including the pathology of attachment trauma and trauma reenactment), and in the family systems constructs of the child's triangulation into the spousal conflict through the formation of a cross-generational coalition with one parent against the other parent.

Professional competence, as defined under Standard 2.01a of the Ethical Principles and Code of Conduct of the American Psychological Association (2002), requires this professional expertise to appropriately and accurately assess, diagnose, and treat this special population of children and families. Failure to possess this requisite professional knowledge may represent practice beyond the boundaries of professional competence, in possible violation of Standard 2.01a of the Ethical Principles and Code of Conduct of the American Psychological Association.

The parent who is providing you with this booklet is concerned that the form of psychopathology described in this booklet is being expressed and enacted in his or her family with his or her children, and this concerned parent is requesting that you assess specifically for this form of psychopathology and document in the patient record the results of this assessment.

Chapter 3

Assessment & Diagnosis

The issue of primary clinical concern is not the highly problematic parenting of the narcissistic/borderline parent per se, but rather the creation of severe child psychopathology as a result of the distorted parenting practices of the narcissistic/borderline parent. When the processes described in this booklet are present, the pathogenic parenting practices of the narcissistic/borderline parent create significant developmental and psychiatric psychopathology in the child which will be evident in the child's symptom display. Aberrant and distorted parenting practices that are inducing significant psychopathology in the child represent pathogenic parenting (i.e., patho=pathology; genic=genesis, creation). To the extent that the pathogenic parenting practices of the narcissistic/borderline parent are producing significant psychopathology in the child, the clinical concerns shift to prominent *child protection* considerations.

Based on the analysis of the pathology provided in *Foundations* (Childress, 2015), the pathogenic parenting practices of the narcissistic/borderline parent will produce a distinctive set of three characteristic diagnostic indicators in the child's symptom display that will reliably identify the pathology, as well as an associated set of additional clinical signs that can be used to support and confirm the diagnosis. The presence in the child's symptom display of the three characteristic diagnostic indicators for the pathogenic parenting associated with an attachment-based model for the construct traditionally referred to as "parental alienation" (as articulated in *Foundations*) would represent definitive clinical evidence for the presence of the pathology described here, and as elaborated in *Foundations* (Childress, 2015).

Diagnostic Indicators

The three diagnostic indicators for an attachment-based model of "parental alienation" (Childress, 2015) are:

1) **Attachment System Suppression:** The child's symptoms evidence a termination of attachment-bonding motivations toward a normal-range and affectionally available parent. The parenting practices of the targeted-rejected parent are assessed to be broadly normal-range with no evidence of serious pathology (i.e., incest, chronic and severe parental violence, chronic and severe parental incapacity) that could reasonably account for the termination of the child's attachment bonding motivation toward this parent.

   Due deference and consideration should be given to the broad spectrum of normal-range parenting practices evident within the general culture, with due consideration given to the legitimate right of parents to define and create family values consistent with their belief systems, and with due consideration given to the normal-range exercise of legitimate parental authority.

2a) **Personality Disorder Symptoms:** The child's symptoms evidence five specific narcissistic/borderline personality traits directed selectively toward the targeted-rejected parent:

   Grandiosity: The child displays a grandiose self-perception of the child's elevated status in the family hierarchy in which the child judges the adequacy of the targeted parent as both a parent and as a person.

   Absence of Empathy: The child displays an absence of empathy for the emotional pain and suffering of the targeted parent. When the child's capacity for empathy toward the targeted parent is explored, the child maintains that the targeted parent "deserves" to be rejected and "deserves" to suffer, or the child denies the authenticity of the parent's hurt and sadness (i.e., the child claims that the parent is "faking" sadness surrounding the child's hostile rejection of this parent).

Entitlement: The child displays an attitude of entitlement relative to the targeted-rejected parent in which the child feels entitled to have his or her desires immediately met by the targeted parent to the child's satisfaction. If, in the child's judgement, the targeted parent does not meet the child's desires to the child's satisfaction, then the child feels entitled to exact a retaliatory revenge on the targeted parent.

Haughty and Arrogant Attitude: The child display an attitude of haughty arrogance and contempt for the targeted-rejected parent. This attitude is selectively displayed toward the targeted-rejected parent, and in other contexts (such as with teachers at school or with the therapist) the child may display a normal-range attitude of respect and well-developed social skills.

Splitting: The child displays a polarized perception regarding his or her parents in which the targeted-rejected parent is perceived as entirely bad whereas the allied and supposedly "favored" narcissistic/borderline parent is reported to be the ideal and all-wonderful parent.

Splitting is also displayed through a rigidity of perception in which relationships and people once defined do not change. According to Linehan (1993), a manifestation of splitting is that "once a person is "flawed," for instance, that person will remain flawed forever" (p. 35). This feature of splitting leads to the associated clinical sign of the child's "non-forgivable grudge" in which the child rigidly maintains that a prior experience with the targeted parent justifies all current and future rejection of the targeted parent.

The child's display of narcissistic and borderline personality traits selectively toward the targeted-rejected parent represents the "psychological fingerprints" in the child's symptom display of parental influence on the child by a narcissistic/borderline parent.

2b) **Anxiety Variant:** In some cases the child will report an excessive and unwarranted anxiety instead of, or in addition to, the narcissistic and borderline symptoms of 2a. In the anxiety variant, the child's anxiety symptoms will meet DSM-5 criteria for a Specific Phobia:

- A *persistent unwarranted fear* of the targeted-rejected parent that is cued either by the presence of the targeted parent or in anticipation of being in the presence of the targeted parent.

- The presence of the targeted-rejected parent almost invariably provokes a *severe anxiety response* which can reach the levels of a situationally provoked panic attack.

- The child seeks to *avoid exposure* to the targeted parent due to the situationally provoked anxiety or else endures the presence of the targeted parent with great distress.

The child's Specific Phobia, however, will be a bizarre and unrealistic "father phobia" or "mother phobia." There is no such thing as a "father phobia" or "mother phobia." This type of phobia does not exist, and so the child's display of a Specific Phobia directed toward a parent is inauthentic and induced.

The child (and the allied narcissistic/borderline) parent may attribute the child's anxiety to a previous negative experience the child had with the targeted parent, in which case the allegation is that the child's phobic anxiety is instead a PTSD response. In evaluating this attribution of the child's reported anxiety, DSM-5 Criterion A for a PTSD diagnosis becomes critical. The creation of PTSD anxiety requires a severe trauma, as defined by the DSM-5 in Criterion A:

> "Exposure to actual or threatened death, serious injury, or sexual violence." (American Psychiatric Association, 2013, p. 271)

Post-traumatic anxiety requires the existence of a trauma of sufficient magnitude to produce *post*-traumatic symptoms. The absence of a trauma of sufficient magnitude to produce post-traumatic symptoms would mean that the child's phobic anxiety relative to a parent is inauthentic and induced rather than the product of an actual trauma experience.

Either diagnostic indicator 2a or 2b is required for a clinical diagnosis of attachment-based "parental alienation" (Childress, 2015).

3) **Delusional Belief:** The child's symptoms display an intransigently held, fixed and false belief (i.e., a delusion) regarding the supposedly "abusive" parental inadequacy of the normal-range and affectionally available targeted parent. The origins of the child's delusional belief is in the child's induced role as the supposedly "victimized child" in the delusional trauma reenactment narrative of the narcissistic/borderline parent. The trauma reenactment narrative is not true. It is a delusional belief of the narcissistic/borderline parent. Therefore, the child's role in this trauma reenactment narrative as the "victimized child" is also a delusional co-creation of the child influenced by the delusional narcissistic/borderline parent.

This child symptom represents a shared delusional belief with the narcissistic/borderline parent in which the parent is the primary case. According to the diagnostic criteria for a shared delusional belief in the DSM-IV TR (a diagnosis no longer available in the DSM-5, although it is still an ICD 10 disorder: F24),

> "Usually the primary case in Shared Psychotic Disorder is dominant in the relationship and gradually imposes the delusional system on the more passive and initially healthy second person. Individuals who come to share

delusional beliefs are often related by blood or marriage and have lived together for a long time, sometimes in relative isolation. If the relationship with the primary case is interrupted, the delusional beliefs of the other individual usually diminish or disappear. Although most commonly seen in relationships of only two people, Shared Psychotic Disorder can occur in larger number of individuals, especially in family situations in which the parent is the primary case and the children, sometimes to varying degrees, adopt the parent's delusional beliefs." (American Psychiatric Association, 2000, p. 333)

The presence of all three diagnostic indicators (*either* 2a or 2b) would represent definitive clinical evidence for the psychological and family processes associated with an attachment-based model for the construct of "parental alienation" as described in *Foundations* (Childress, 2015). If the diagnostic indicators for a clinical diagnosis of an attachment-based model of parental alienation are present, the appropriate DSM-5 diagnosis would be:

DSM-5 Diagnosis

    309.4   Adjustment Disorder with mixed disturbance of emotions and conduct

    V61.20 Parent-Child Relational Problem

    V61.29 Child Affected by Parental Relationship Distress

    V995.51 Child Psychological Abuse, Confirmed

The rationale for the DSM-5 diagnosis of V995.51 Child Psychological Abuse, Confirmed is provided in *Foundations* (Childress, 2015). Pathogenic parenting practices that involve a *role-reversal* exploitation of the child as a "regulatory object" to stabilize and regulate the pathology of the narcissistic/borderline parent, in which significant developmental,[5] personality disorder,[6]

---

[5] the induced suppression of the normal-range functioning of the child's attachment system.

[6] five specific narcissistic and borderline personality disorder traits.

and psychiatric[7] symptoms are being created in the child, and which causes the child to lose a bonded relationship with a normal-range and affectionally available parent, represents a form of child psychological abuse. Both the nature and the severity of the child's pathology which is created by the pathogenic parenting practices of the narcissistic/borderline parent elevate the clinical concerns to those of child protection considerations (Childress, 2015).

Additional Clinical Signs

The pathology of attachment-based "parental alienation," as described in *Foundations* (Childress, 2015), also predicts a priori a set of associated clinical features, even to the use of specific words and phrases. While these associated clinical signs are not definitive diagnostic indicators of the pathology, these associated clinical signs are correlated psychological features. These associated clinical signs include the following clinical features and displays:

Child Empowerment

The pathology is reflected in ongoing efforts by the allied and supposedly "favored" parent to empower the child's active agency in rejecting the targeted parent by advocating that "the child be allowed to decide whether or not to go on visitations" with the other parent, and that therapists and the court should "listen to the child" regarding what the child wants. The emphasis on child empowerment represents both a corrective change to the original childhood trauma experience of the narcissistic/borderline parent (Childress, 2015), and is also a characteristic indicator of the role-reversal relationship inherent to the pathology in which the narcissistic/borderline parent seeks to empower the child's rejection of the other parent in order to exploit the child and the child's symptoms to meet the needs of the parent.

---

[7] phobic anxiety and delusional beliefs.

Of particular concern, and characteristic of the pathology, are efforts by the allied and supposedly "favored" parent to have the child testify in court in order to express rejection of the other parent. The effort to empower the child to testify in court in order to reject a parent represents a profound absence of empathy for the child's authentic experience and is characteristic of severely narcissistic parenting and a role-reversal relationship. Whenever a parent seeks to have a child testify in court in order to reject the other parent, the possibility of pathogenic parenting associated with an attachment-based model of "parental alienation" should immediately be considered and assessed.

The Term "Abuse"

The use of the terms "abuse" or "abusive" by the allied and supposedly "favored" parent to *inaccurately* characterize the parenting practices of the other parent is highly characteristic of how narcissistic and borderline personalities describe unfavorable relationships. Normal-range personalities tend to use less inflammatory and hyperbolic terms, such as rude, mean, inconsiderate, horrible, etc. to describe other people's actions, but rarely do they characterize unfavorable treatment as "abuse," except in situations of authentic abuse. All allegations of child abuse and domestic violence must be taken seriously and fully investigated. In addition, the use of the specific words "abuse" and "abusive" to characterize the actions of other people is also particularly characteristic of narcissistic and borderline personality processes and should be considered as a possible differential diagnostic indicator within a broader context of signs and symptoms when a thorough investigation of the allegations does not reveal authentic abuse.

The Term "Forced"

Both the narcissistic/borderline parent and the child will use the specific word "forced" to characterize the child being asked to cooperate in visitation and contact with the other parent.

> N/B Parent: "The child shouldn't be *forced* to go on visitations with the other parent."

N/B Parent: "I can't *force* the child to talk with the other parent."

Child: "I don't want to be *forced* to go on visitations with the other parent. I'm not ready. Maybe when I'm ready."

The child's use of the phrase, "I'm not ready," particularly in conjunction with the use of the word "force" is particularly characteristic of the pathology. In actuality, the child is being asked to *cooperate* in showing and receiving loving affection from a normal-range and affectionally available parent. The child is essentially saying that he or she doesn't want to be "forced" to receive a parent's love and affection, and isn't "ready" to be loved by a parent. Love and loving are not bad things. This statement by the child is bizarre and indicates the inauthentic origins of this symptom characteristic.

Display of the "Protective Parent" Role

Conspicuous displays by the allied and supposedly "favored" parent of the coveted role as the all-wonderful protective parent (e.g., "I only want what's best for the child"), including the display of protective behaviors (e.g., unnecessarily providing the child with food or clothing to take to the other parent's home) or "retrieval behaviors" (e.g., excessive or hidden phone calls, texts, and emails to the child when the child is in the care of the other parent), and expressed but unspecified concerns for the child's "safety" in being with the other parent, are all characteristic clinical signs of this pathology.

Child Placed Out Front

The allied and supposedly "favored" parent places the child in the leadership position of rejecting a relationship with the other parent, particularly at visitation transfers, and then adopts a "helpless stance" of selective parental incompetence (e.g., "What can I do, I can't make the child go on visitations with the other parent"). This symptom characteristic is indicative of the role-reversal relationship in which the narcissistic/borderline parent is *inducing* and then *exploiting* the child's elicited symptoms while hiding behind the child. A characteristic phrase stem used by the narcissistic/borderline parent is, "It's not me, it's the child who…"

> **N/B Parent:** "It's not me, it's the child who doesn't want the other parent at the child's music recital (school activity, sports game, etc.)."

> **N/B Parent:** "I tell the child to be nice and cooperate with the other parent, but what can I do, I can't *force* the child to be nice. It's not me, it's the child. And in truth, I know just what the child is going through, the other parent was just like that with me during our marriage. But it's not me, I tell the child to cooperate; it's the child."

> **N/B Parent:** "It's not me, it's the child who's afraid. I tell the child to try not to be afraid, that if something bad happens with the other parent the child can always call me and I'll come and get them, but the child is just so afraid of the other parent. But it's not me, it's the child who's afraid. And I worry about the child's safety too, but what can I do, I have to follow the court orders."

Shared Victimization

The allied and supposedly "favored" parent and child support each other in their bond of "shared victimization" by the targeted-rejected parent (e.g., "I know just what the child is going through, the other parent treated me the same way during our marriage"). This symptom feature represents the diffusion of psychological boundaries between the identity and experience of the child and the identity and experience of the parent. As a result of the role-reversal relationship and the psychological needs of the narcissistic/borderline parent, the child has become a narcissistic reflection for the attitudes and beliefs of the narcissistic/borderline parent. This fusion of psychological states is then used by the narcissistic/borderline parent as supposed evidence for the veracity of their shared belief, when in truth it simply represents the nullification of the child's separate authenticity in order to adopt and reflect the beliefs of the parent.

Repeated Disregard of Court Orders

The allied and supposedly "favored" parent repeatedly disregards court orders for visitation and custody, which then requires that the targeted-rejected parent repeatedly return to court to seek enforcement of prior court orders. This diagnostic sign is associated with the inability of the narcissistic and borderline personality structure to conform to external expectations and restrictions on their behavior and impulses. According to Beck et al. (2004),

> Narcissistic individuals also use power and entitlement as evidence of superiority... As a means of demonstrating their power, narcissists may alter boundaries, make unilateral decisions, control others, and determine exceptions to rules that apply to other, ordinary people. (p. 251)

The narcissistic and borderline personality simply lacks the structure needed to limit and control impulses. As a result, restrictions on the narcissistic/borderline personality imposed by court orders are essentially rendered meaningless by the narcissistic sense of entitlement and the general incapacity of the narcissistic/borderline personality structure to limit and restrain their impulses.

Characteristic Themes for the Child's Rejection

A set of typical themes for the child's rejection of a relationship with the targeted parent represent projections of narcissistic personality traits onto the other parent. These projections are being acquired by the child through the influence of the narcissistic/borderline parent.

The Insensitive Parent

> "My mother is so self-centered, she always thinks of herself, she never considers what other people want."

> "It always has to be his way. My dad never does what I want to do."

Parental Anger Management

"My dad gets angry about the littlest things. He has anger management problems."

"My mother can't control her temper. She's always getting angry over nothing."

The Parent Doesn't Take Responsibility

"My mother/(father) never apologies for what she does wrong. She doesn't take responsibility for anything *she* does wrong."

This attribution of causality can sometimes lead to naïve therapists seeking a parental apology to the child, which drastically inverts a healthy parent-child hierarchy, empowers the child into judging the parent, legitimizes the child's distorted account of events, and never acts to restore the parent-child relationship.

Within the pathology, this attribution for the child's rejection of the targeted parent reflects the projection onto the targeted parent of the narcissistic/borderline parent's propensity to externalize blame and never take responsibility, and reflects this theme provided to the child by the narcissistic/borderline parent's judgement of the targeted parent as being to blame (for everything).

Vague Personhood of the Parent

"I don't know, it's just something about the way my mother says stuff... it's so irritating... like her tone of voice or something."

"My dad just bothers me. He'll ask me questions and things. It's just annoying. I just want him to leave me alone."

New Romantic Relationship of the Parent

The theme is that the targeted parent is neglecting the child by not giving the child enough attention because of the parent's new romantic relationship or time spent with the new spouse. This theme emerges from the desire of the narcissistic/borderline parent to intrude into and disrupt the other parent's new romantic relationship. The child is being used (role-reversal relationship as the "regulatory object" for the parent) as the means to disrupt the targeted parent's new romantic relationship.

"He's always spending time with his new wife. He doesn't spend enough special time with just me." (with the implied extension of "... so that's why I *never* want to see this parent again, because I want *more* special time with this parent." This is illogical on its face, but it is consistent with the irrational thinking of a narcissistic/borderline process).

The Non-forgivable Grudge

"I can't forgive my mother for what she did in the past. I just can't get over what happened in the past."

"My father deserves being rejected for what he did in the past."

The assertion or implication that the targeted parent "deserves" to be punished for some past failure as a parent/(person) is highly characteristic of this pathology.

Prior Parental Absence and Non-Involvement

This theme alleges that the child's current rejection of the targeted parent is due to the parent's prior non-involvement with the child. The child is essentially alleging that the child was so hurt by the prior parental non-involvement that the child no longer wants the involvement of the parent (i.e., essentially the child is seeking revenge on the parent for the parent's supposed prior non-involvement).

This allegation is also illogical on its face. If the child is hurt by the targeted parent's prior non-involvement, this supposed hurt means that the child WANTS the involvement of the targeted parent (and is hurt because it was not available). If this is true, it is easily solvable. We can simply give the child copious amounts of parental involvement now from this parent to make it up to the child. But this is exactly what is being rejected by the child, which doesn't make sense.

In actuality, this symptom feature represents a projection of the neglect the narcissistic/borderline parent feels as a spouse (i.e., "the other spouse didn't give me the attention I deserved") and the hostile retaliation and revenge motive of the narcissistic/borderline parent (expressed and enacted by the child through the child's role-reversal relationship).

Vacancy of Attachment Bond

The child displays an absence of possessive ownership for the targeted parent. The child may refer to the targeted parent by the parent's first name rather than "mom" or "dad," or the child may begin calling the new step-parent spouse of the narcissistic/borderline parent "mother" or "father."

The attachment system is very specific and strongly confers feelings of possessive ownership onto the attachment figure; *my* mother, *my* father, *my* husband, *my* wife; that person *belongs* to me and I *belong* to that person. People are not interchangeable. In the evolution of the attachment system, if the child ran to any member of the social group in response to a predator threat the child may or may not receive protection from the predator. If, on the other hand, the child sought the protection of a *specific* person of the parent (*my* mother; *my* father), the person who *belonged* to the child, then the child was more likely to receive protection and so would be more likely to survive. The possessive ownership of the parent is a deeply embedded feature of the attachment system.

For a child to reject possessive ownership of a parent, or to "replace" a parent with a "new parent," is extremely bizarre and is inauthentic to the functioning of the attachment system. However, the replaceability of people is a characteristic feature of narcissistic and borderline personalities. According to Kernberg (1975), when the other person no longer provides narcissistic gratification they are "dropped and dismissed because there was no real capacity for love of this object in the first place" (p. 33).

However, the authentic attachment bond is irreplaceable. As described by Mary Ainsworth (1989), one of the leading authorities on the nature and functioning of the attachment system, an attached relationship is "a relatively long-enduring tie in which the partner is important as a unique individual and is *interchangeable with none other*" (p. 711, emphasis added). The vacancy of the child's possessive ownership of a parent is an extremely unusual and aberrant child symptom, and yet it is highly characteristic of the pathology described in this booklet and in *Foundations* (Childress, 2015).

The Exclusion Demand

The child demands that the targeted parent no long attend the child's activities, such as sporting events, school activities, award ceremonies, music and dance recitals, etc. The child alleges that the presence of the targeted parent at these events creates stress for the child and distracts the child's focus away from the activity. The targeted parent is thereby excluded from even being present to watch the child's life unfold (i.e., an ex-parent as well as an ex-spouse).

The source of this exclusion demand is the child's role-reversal relationship with the narcissistic/borderline parent. It is actually the narcissistic/borderline parent who is distressed by the other parent's attendance at the child's activities. The child is merely acting as a "regulatory object" to maintain the emotional and psychological state of the narcissistic/borderline parent. When the targeted parent attends the child's activities the narcissistic/borderline parent becomes emotionally distressed and signals a potential collapse into an emotionally dysregulated state.

As the external "regulatory object" for the narcissistic/borderline parent, the child's role is to keep the narcissistic/borderline parent in an organized and regulated emotional state. The threatened collapse of the narcissistic/borderline parent into emotional dysregulation is anxiety provoking and stressful for the child, who must then respond in ways that keep the narcissistic/borderline parent in an organized and regulated state.

The source of the child's stress is not the targeted parent per se, it is the impact that the targeted parent's presence has on the narcissistic/borderline parent and the child's role-reversal need to keep the narcissistic/borderline parent in an organized and regulated state. The child is excluding the targeted parent because the presence of the targeted parent distresses the narcissistic/borderline parent and threatens to collapse this parent's emotional regulation. By excluding the targeted parent from the child's activities, the child is acting as a "regulatory object" for the needs of the narcissistic/borderline parent, who is the actual source of the desire to exclude the targeted parent from the child's life (i.e., to make the ex-spouse an ex-parent as well).

The child, however, doesn't accurately understand and interpret the source of the stress, and simply experiences the presence of the targeted parent as somehow being stressful. The child simply knows that he or she becomes more stressed when the targeted parent is at the child's events than when the targeted parent does not attend. The "exclusion demand" by the child is a particularly characteristic feature of this pathology and the role-reversal relationship with the allied and supposedly "favored" parent ("It's not me, it's the child who is excluding the other parent").

Diagnostic Checklist

A diagnostic checklist for documenting the presence of the three diagnostic indicators of attachment-based "parental alienation" and the associated clinical signs is available from the professional website of Dr. Childress at: drcachildress.org and can also be requested from the parent who is providing you with this booklet.

Professional Competence

The parent who is providing you with this booklet is concerned that the pathology described in this booklet, and which is more fully elaborated in *Foundations* (Childress, 2015), is occurring with his or her child and in the surrounding family context. This parent is simply asking that mental health professionals who are assessing, diagnosing, and treating this parent's children and family consider the pathology described in this booklet and to then specifically assess for this pathology.

The nature of this pathology represents the trans-generational transmission of attachment trauma through the reenactment of a false and constructed narrative of supposed "abuse" and "victimization," which is mediated by the pathology of narcissistic and borderline personality dynamics involving projection and splitting, and involves the child's triangulation into the spousal conflict through the formation of a cross-generational coalition of the child with the narcissistic/borderline parent against the normal-range and affectionally available targeted parent. Both the nature of the pathology and its complexity warrant the designation of these children and families as representing a *"special population"* who require specialized professional knowledge and expertise to competently assess, diagnose, and treat.

Domains of Specialized Professional Knowledge

Attachment Theory

The appropriate assessment, diagnosis and treatment of this pathology requires an expert professional understanding for the attachment system (Bowlby, 1969, 1973; 1980), including the impact of childhood attachment trauma on the subsequent formation of personality disorder processes (e.g., Fonagy, Target, Gergely, Allen, & Bateman, 2003), the characteristic patterns of insecure child attachment to problematic parenting (e.g., Bretherton, 1992), the reenactment of internal working models of attachment trauma in current relationships (e.g., Pearlman & Courtois, 2005; van der Kolk, 1989), and the characteristics of normal range and distorted expressions of children's attachment motivations across the various age levels.

Personality Disorders

The appropriate assessment, diagnosis and treatment of this pathology also requires an expert professional understanding for the psychological and interpersonal dynamics of narcissistic and borderline personality processes, including an understanding for the psychological decompensation of narcissistic and borderline personality structures into delusional belief systems under stress (e.g., Millon, 2011), the projective and splitting dynamics associated with narcissistic and borderline personality processes (e.g., Kernberg, 1975), the role-reversal relationship use of the child as a "regulatory object" for the parent (e.g., Kerig, 2005), the "invalidating environment" as described by Linehan (1993) that nullifies authentic child self-experience, and an advanced professional expertise in the clinical recognition of narcissistic and borderline personality dynamics within the clinical interview setting (e.g., Beck et al, 2004).

Family Systems Theory

The appropriate assessment, diagnosis and treatment of this pathology requires an expert level of professional understanding for family systems constructs of the child's triangulation into the spousal conflict through the formation of a cross-generational coalition of the child with one parent against the other parent (e.g., Haley, 1977; Minuchin, 1974) and for the symptom indicators of a cross-generational parent-child coalition.

Acquiring Professional Competence

This specialized professional knowledge can be acquired from the cited source material and from professional experience in assessing, diagnosing, and treating attachment system distortions, personality disorder dynamics, shared delusional belief systems, and cross-generational coalitions within the family system. The characteristic pathology of an attachment-based model for the construct of "parental alienation" is also elaborated more fully in the book *Foundations* (Childress, 2015), which can also be used as a basis for establishing professional competence with this special population of children and families.

The child's parent has a right defined under Standard 2.01a of the Ethical Principles and Code of Conduct for the American Psychological Association to expect professional competence in the assessment, diagnosis, and treatment of his or her child and family. Failure to possess the requisite professional knowledge to appropriately and accurately assess, diagnose, and treat the pathology of this special population of children and families may represent practice beyond the boundaries of professional competence in violation of Standard 2.01a of the Ethical Principles and Code of Conduct for the American Psychological Association.

If, as a result of practice beyond the boundaries of professional competence, developmental and psychological harm then accrues to the child, and emotional and psychological harm is inflicted on the targeted-rejected parent from a failure to appropriately assess, diagnose, and treat the pathology involved with this family, then this may also represent a violation of Standard 3.04 of the Ethical Principles and Code of Conduct for the American Psychological Association regarding Avoiding Harm to the client. In addition, a professional failure to identify and accurately diagnose the psychological child abuse involved in the creation of significant developmental and psychiatric pathology in the child through the distorted and pathogenic parenting practices of a narcissistic/borderline parent may also represent a failure in the professional duty to protect.

Assessing & Documenting the Pathology

The parent who is providing you with this booklet is concerned about both the nature and the severity of the pathology which is being expressed by his or her child and in the surrounding family context, and this parent is simply seeking an appropriate assessment, diagnosis, and treatment of the pathology that will restore the child's normal-range and healthy development.

Determining the nature of the pathology within any family is dependent on a variety of factors and will be determined based on a thorough clinical assessment. All the parent who is providing you with this booklet is seeking is your consideration of the possible pathology described in this booklet (elaborated more fully in *Foundations*) and documentation in the patient record regarding the results of a clinical assessment for this possible pathology.

If the three diagnostic indicators of the pathology described in this booklet are present, then I ask that you to make an appropriate DSM-5 diagnosis of the pathology, including the warranted DSM-5 diagnosis of V995.51 Child Psychological Abuse, Confirmed. If, on the other hand, the three diagnostic indicators of this pathology are not present, then simply document the results of the assessment in the patient's record regarding which diagnostic indicators were not present, and make an appropriate DSM-5 diagnosis based on the nature of the symptom features displayed.

References

Ainsworth, M.D.S. (1989). Attachments beyond infancy. American Psychologist, 44, 709-716.

American Psychiatric Association. (2000). Diagnostic and statistical manual of mental disorders (Revised 4th ed.). Washington, DC: Author.

American Psychiatric Association. (2013). Diagnostic and statistical manual of mental disorders (5th ed.). Washington, DC: Author.

American Psychological Association. (2002). American Psychological Association ethical principles of psychologists and code of conduct. Retrieved March 1, 2015, from http://www.apa.org/ethics/code2002.html

Bailey, J.M. and Shriver, A. (1999). Does childhood sexual abuse cause borderline personality disorder? Journal of Sex & Marital Therapy, 25, 45-57)

Beck, A.T., Freeman, A., Davis, D.D., and Associates (2004). Cognitive therapy of personality disorders. (2nd edition). New York: Guilford.

Bowlby, J. (1969). Attachment and Loss: Vol. 1. Attachment. NY: Basic Books.

Bowlby, J. (1973). Attachment and Loss: Vol. 2. Separation: Anxiety and Anger. NY: Basic Books.

Bowlby, J. (1980). Attachment and Loss: Vol. 3. Loss: Sadness and Depression. NY: Basic Books.

Bretherton, I. (1992). The origins of attachment theory: John Bowlby and Mary Ainsworth. Developmental Psychology, 1992, 28, 759-775.

Childress, C.A. (2015). An attachment-based model of parental alienation: Foundations. Claremont, CA: Oaksong Press.

Fonagy, P., Target, M., Gergely, G., Allen, J.G., and Bateman, A. W. (2003). The developmental roots of Borderline Personality Disorder in early attachment relationships: A theory and some evidence. Psychoanalytic Inquiry, 23, 412-459.

Haley, J. (1977). Tofward a theory of pathological systems. In P. Watzlawick & J. Weakland (Eds.), The interactional view (pp. 31-48). New York: Norton.

Juni, S. (1995). Triangulation as splitting in the service of ambivalence. Current Psychology: Research and Reviews, 14, 91-111.

Kernberg, O.F. (1975). Borderline conditions and pathological narcissism. New York: Aronson.

Linehan, M. M. (1993). Cognitive-behavioral treatment of borderline personality disorder. New York, NY: Guilford

Millon. T. (2011). Disorders of personality: introducing a DSM/ICD spectrum from normal to abnormal. Hoboken: Wiley.

Minuchin, S. (1974). Families and family therapy. Harvard University Press.

Pearlman, C.A., Courtois, C.A. (2005). Clinical Applications of the Attachment Framework: Relational Treatment of Complex Trauma. Journal of Traumatic Stress, 18, 449-459.

Prager, J. (2003). Lost childhood, lost generations: the intergenerational transmission of trauma. Journal of Human Rights, 2, 173-181.

Rappoport, A. (2005). Co-narcissism: How we accommodate to narcissistic parents. *The Therapist*.

van der Kolk, B.A. (1989). The compulsion to repeat the trauma: Re-enactment, revictimization, and masochism. Psychiatric Clinics of North America, 12, 389-411

ABOUT THE AUTHOR

Dr. Childress is a licensed clinical psychologist currently in private practice in Pasadena, California. He teaches graduate level courses in Models of Psychotherapy, Assessment and Treatment Planning, Diagnosis and Psychopathology, Research Methods, and Child Development. Prior to entering private practice, Dr. Childress served as the Clinical Director for an early childhood assessment and treatment center primarily working with children in the foster care system. The clinical focus of Dr. Childress is child and family therapy, the treatment of Attention Deficit Hyperactivity Disorder (ADHD), angry and oppositional children, parent-child conflicts, parenting, and marital problems. He also has an additional clinical expertise in early childhood mental health, with a focus on the socially mediated neurodevelopment of the brain during childhood.

Made in the USA
Columbia, SC
02 April 2019